BRITAIN IN PICTURES
THE BRITISH PEOPLE IN PICTURES

ENGLISH
COTTAGES AND FARM-HOUSES

GENERAL EDITOR
W. J. TURNER

The Editor is most grateful to all those who have
so kindly helped in the selection of illustrations
especially to officials of the various public
Museums Libraries and Galleries and
to all others who have generously
allowed pictures and MSS
to be reproduced

ENGLISH COTTAGES
AND FARM-HOUSES

C. HENRY WARREN

*WITH
8 PLATES IN COLOUR
AND
27 ILLUSTRATIONS IN
BLACK & WHITE*

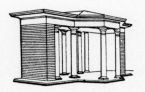

COLLINS · 14 ST. JAMES'S PLACE · LONDON
MCMXLVIII

PRODUCED BY
ADPRINT LIMITED LONDON

PRINTED IN GREAT BRITAIN BY
CLARKE & SHERWELL LTD NORTHAMPTON
ON MELLOTEX BOOK PAPER MADE BY
TULLIS RUSSELL & CO LTD MARKINCH SCOTLAND

FARM COTTAGES.

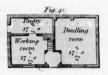

LIST OF ILLUSTRATIONS

PLATES IN COLOUR

BLACK AND WHITE ILLUSTRATIONS

AT SANDPIT GATE, WINDSOR: INTERIOR
Water colour by Paul Sandby, 1725-1809

OF TWO FARM-HOUSES, WEST AND EAST

IT is more than an expression of idle sentiment to say that old houses seem to have developed through the years an individuality—even, if you prefer it, a personality. Something clings to them from the lives of those who have inhabited them. This is most true, of course, where the house has been in the possession of the same family for generations. Gradually it has shaped itself to the character of its successive occupiers, until they almost seem to live on, after a fashion, in the place that was always home to them.

Especially is this the case with old farm-houses. The mere continuity of the life and work which they have known, season after season, generation after generation, somehow renders them peculiarly susceptible to the imprint of their inmates' personalities. Mansions, however long they may

7

have been in the same family, are perhaps too big, too impersonal, for such subtle imprint to have an obvious effect: their history links them to the great world outside and needs the elucidation of a guide. And cottages mostly change hands too often. But it is nothing for a farm-house to remain in the same family for a hundred, and more than a hundred, years. The sea is not more zealous of the sailor than the land is of the farmer: it will not let him go. And so the farm gets passed on from father to son through the generations, each one of which, changing with the changing fashion, leaves its individual mark upon the pile of stones and wood, bricks and mortar, which it called home.

There is an old farm-house in the West Country where the imprint of its owners has always seemed to me peculiarly plain to see. It is approached through a maze of quiet lanes, the last of which, leading directly up to the house, is little better than a river of mud for the greater part of the year. And its remoteness is further emphasised by the fact that the house turns its back on the lane and sets its eyes on the hills. It is built of stone, weathered to the kindest hue, and its tiles are of stone also. It follows the favourite L-shaped pattern, embracing a cobbled yard where the activities of house and farm intimately mingle. Everything here, as indoors, tells a story. Outmoded implements of all kinds overflow from the sheds; and one day, disturbing the weeds underneath a tree, I came upon the broad, turned-up blade of an old breast-plough. Even the soft-water tub by the back door is really an immense brewing copper, with wide lip, whose heady contents once helped to assuage the thirst of the summer reapers.

Here, as in all farm-houses, the kitchen is the focus and centre of the whole life of the place. And yet there is a notable difference. It is as if, forty or fifty years ago, time had stood still; and indeed, for reasons which it were pointless to enlarge upon now, that is very much what did happen to this old farm-house. If, for instance, the kitchen were to be transferred to a museum, just as it is to-day, it would serve as a model of any substantial farm-house kitchen of years ago.

Everything therein is strong and plain and most durable, from the great scrubbed elm table occupying the middle of the room to the dresser that fills the whole of one wall. The rough usage of men coming in from the fields made it essential that plainness should come before ornament here, strength before beauty. There are no coverings on the stone-slabbed floor, so that the room continually resounds with the tapping of feet and the scraping of chairs. The oaken beams of the ceiling have been white-washed and beneath them, over the table, is suspended a rack which can be lowered at will and is a handy receptacle for guns. The only colour in the place is provided by the china on the dresser and, in summer, by the two enormous pots of scarlet geraniums that flare on the little patch of grass immediately outside the window.

8

SINGERS FARM, NEAR BUSHEY IN HERTFORDSHIRE
Water colour by Henry Edridge, 1811

THE OUTHOUSE

Water colour by William Henry Hunt, 1790–1864

But if the kitchen is the core of the farm-house, the wide, open hearth is the core of the kitchen. Not even in the heat of mid-summer is the fire allowed to go out. Always there is a pile of sparking ashes and across it a smouldering log. Against a soot-encrusted fire-back one or two kettles are always on the boil where they hang on pot-hooks suspended from an old chimney crane. Ranged along the high mantel-piece above them are candlesticks and horn lanterns, a tinder-box and even a dinted old leaden tobacco-jar. And then, to complete the scene, there is a long, curved settle, shiny with use, placed so as to keep out the draughts from the scullery. For of course, like all farm-houses, this one is always ablow.

A couple of stone steps lead down into the dairy. This, since lattices take the place of windows, is blowier than ever. White and cool and clean, it suggests even now the quantities of milk and cream and butter which were once its daily traffic; but the great pans, spaced along the slate slab shelves, are empty and the churn stands idle in a corner. On one of the window-sills, unwanted any more, are butter-markers—the mark in this case being a design of lovers' knots. Only the long trestle-table is in use still, its well-filled dishes and basins covered with yards of muslin. Properly speaking this room should be called the larder; but, though it has long lost its original use, it will never lose its original name.

Overhead are the bedrooms of the family and those other bedrooms—now lumber-rooms only—where once upon a time the bachelor farm-hands slept. Apples and pears lie tumbled over the floors; and if the mice play havoc with some, what matter, since there are so many of one sort and another that even in March and April you could come up here and help yourself to a basketful of sound and wholesome fruit? In the used bedrooms the floors sometimes alter their level, from centre to side, by as much as six inches, so that there is one place only where each piece of furniture can stand more or less firm. The doors, though there are gaps top and bottom, are made secure with wooden latches that clatter with every coming and going, and the windows, with their leaded panes, rattle with every bit of wind. In such airy rooms a four-poster bed, complete with its hangings, is more than ornamental and there is one here. And on the walls are pious pictures, in glossy unreality, and even more pious texts, florally entwined.

The front door opens straight into the kitchen, and thither one advances, instinctively, on entering; but sometimes, on festive occasions or birthdays or visits from new-comers, one is gently guided in a contrary direction, towards the dining-room.

I do not know the words that could do this old dining-room full justice; and anyhow, if I were to set down in detail everything it contains, I doubt if I should be believed. From the huge mahogany table in the centre, spread with damask and decorated with a tinted glass epergne of elaborate design, to the so solid sideboard with its load of silver-plate and glass, it bespeaks a permanence, an assurance of continuing generations, such as only our Victorian fathers would have dared to envisage. Here, in contrast to the plain, white-washed kitchen, a rich red wall-paper is hung with portraits of the family and an oil painting or two of a prize stallion or a nationally famous ox. The fire-place—an open grate this time—is filled in summer with green boughs and in winter with enough firing to keep a cottage warm through a whole week. Nevertheless, though the faces of those sitting round it may burn till they are red, back and sides go ever cold; for even here draughts abound. Culture is represented by a single shelf of books, mostly religious or agricultural and all old and unused; whilst on the fringed and tasselled mantel-piece a couple of spotted Staffordshire dogs smile in china imbecility on the scene below.

Finally there is the parlour. This is the sanctum sanctorum and I have never even heard of its being used: I should not think anybody would dare. Not that the air is musty or that dust is allowed to accumulate. It is kept spotless, but not for use. All that is delicate and rare among the family belongings has been placed here: china that chimes on the finger-nail, ornaments that solved somebody's problem of a wedding present, boxes inlaid with mother-o'-pearl, chairs so frail no farmer would be safe sitting on them, snow-scenes under glass, antimacassars and embroidered shawls, and even a spinet whose yellowing keys either give forth a faraway sound or no sound at all.

But such a farm-house as this is not to be found down every English lane. Indeed, my purpose in describing it, even so superficially, has not been to show what our farm-houses are like to-day, but rather to try and give a hint of what they were like yesterday—or at least the more prosperous of them. So let me set against this picture (admittedly and necessarily a still-life at best) another picture of a farm-house the other side of the country; one that is no less old and no less interesting; but one where time has certainly not stood still.

The farm-house I have in mind this time is situated in East Anglia. It is every bit as remote as its West Country fellow, but the narrow chace that leads to it is well made and kept (at the farmer's expense) and even the hedges that line it are as neatly trimmed as a garden's. I like that first view of the house from the chace, especially in early Spring, when the cherry-plum is in blossom and the yellow-washed walls of plaster are netted over with a tracery of shadow-boughs. It stands high, a vantage point from which the farmer can view most of his fields at a glance; and a cluster of fine old trees protect it from the prevailing wind.

The nearer one approaches, the clearer it becomes—as one had guessed from the start—that here is a well-cared-for farm. It is one, moreover, where the advantages of progress have not been scorned. In the open sheds near the stack-yard, for instance, there are, besides numerous other implements, three tractors of recent date. And evidently the farmer believes

FARMYARD SCENE IN THE SEVENTEENTH CENTURY
Ink drawing by Francis Barlow, *c.* 1626-1702

in having his own tackle wherever possible, rather than in being dependent upon the inconveniences and consequent losses of borrowing, for there is also a threshing drum. But what are those two monster steam engines doing there? They are the "black horses," as the steam plough is called in these parts. Covered with tarpaulins, they are seldom used to-day but they must have been an expensive innovation when they first came rumbling up the chace. Then again, hard by the old barn, with its decent weather-boarding outside and its superb oak within, stand two Dutch barns. Some people, I know, would protest that these latter are ugly and out of keeping; but I do not see them this way. To me, quite apart from the considerable comeliness of their line, they represent a progressive contribution to the agricultural architecture of our time—like the silo and the caterpillar trac-tor and the combine harvester; and I would think little of an artist who avoided the discipline of integrating them in his pictures of the rural scene to-day. Anyway, there they are; and in fact, wherever one goes on this farm, the old and the new are to be seen in happy juxtaposition—the certain indication in its owner of an open, if still cautious, mind.

11

But let us leave the out-buildings and go across to the farm-house itself. Here, again, is the favourite L-shaped plan. Swing open the little gate and you enter a court-yard where in scattered coops the hens are gently clucking to their broods and a dozen Aylesbury ducks, white as a Monday's wash, come slowly up from the pond. These are the care of the farmer's wife. So, too, are the turkeys and geese; the eggs which she washes and sells to the dealer; and the butter which she makes once a week. She may be, like her husband, progressive; but she is not so progressive that she cannot fulfil the proper role of a farmer's wife as Tusser understood it more than three hundred years ago.

Before going indoors, take a closer look at this court-yard and the garden beyond. Farmers, it is said, make bad gardeners; but here at least is one farmer to disprove this facile adage. All the sun gathers to this little yard; and he has set his best trees against its walls, including a peach and an apricot whose fruit can be plucked leaning out of the bedroom windows. A fair-sized patch of grass provides a handy drying-ground for the week's laundry that flaps above frames full of early salads. Beyond is the garden proper, as well-stocked as any cottager's and with much more variety. Fruit-trees are perhaps this farmer's speciality; and if he has inherited good from his fathers, he has planted even better for his children. Pears hang against the barns, plums against the house; hens scrabble under damsons and bullaces. There is fruit everywhere.

As for the interior of the farm-house, I think Richard Jefferies must have had just such a place in mind when he wrote of his old Wiltshire home. "The kitchen had perhaps originally been the house, the rest having been added to it in the course of years as the mode of life changed and increasing civilisation demanded more convenience and comfort." And thus it was, no doubt, in this East Anglian farm-house too. Kitchen, scullery, dairy, brew-house and bake-house are all gathered into one wing, whilst the other, newer, more spacious, more pretentious in a way, is taken up with a large drawing-room, a hall, and bedrooms over. The kitchen may look on to the court-yard, with its dog-kennels and hen-coops, its squeaky pump and its clothes-line posts; but the large french windows of the drawing-room look on to a spacious lawn, with its feathery pampas-grass and roses and trim, circular beds of annuals. It is almost as if there were two houses in one: this for work and that for play.

All the same, there is no doubt where the real heart of the house is. If this particular East Anglian kitchen is no match, for (shall I say ?) historic interest, with the West Country one, it is every bit as much the core and focus of the place. Here the farmer's wife spends most of her time —too much, she might well protest. Here the dealer, the grocer, the baker, the higgler and all the rest of them call, bringing gossip from the outside world as well as merchandise, and as likely as not wetting their whistles with a cup of cider or beer. And here the farmer himself chats with his

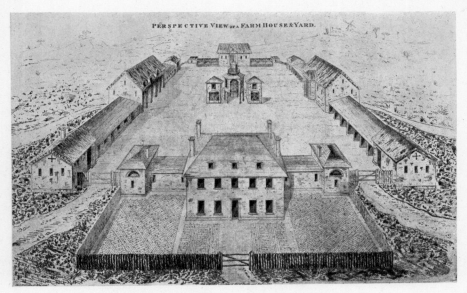

PERSPECTIVE VIEW OF A FARM-HOUSE AND YARD
Engraving from Charles Middleton's *Picturesque and Architectural Views*, 1795

friends and neighbours, hurries over his mid-day meal, dozes over his paper in the evening—never venturing into the drawing-room until Sunday brings more leisure and cleaner clothes.

You will find here no curious relics of yesterday, no tinder-boxes or settles or chimney cranes: all have been swept away as new needs brought in new fashions. A petroleum lamp stands on the dresser. A cleaned-out fireplace is filled with a Calor gas stove. The brew-house has been fitted up with wash-basin and racks and pegs for the men's dirty clothes and boots. A window has been put in over the sink, so that the farmer's wife may have something else to look at besides soap-suds and tea-leaves—and, incidentally, may watch to see who is coming up the lane and keep an eye on the heifers in the meadow across the way. Altogether, it is as clear here as it was in the farm-yard that this is a farm-house where the occupiers, in contradiction to the usual conservatism of their kind, have moved with the times.

Cobbett, in his reactionary and conservative way, would even say—and in no uncertain terms—that the farmer's wife had moved too much with the times. What has a farmer's wife to do with fancy drawing-rooms complete with occasional tables and china cabinets and expensive rugs, and even a piano? But I think Jefferies showed a far saner attitude when he said that the problem is "how to enjoy the intellectual progress of the

13

FARMYARD AT THETFORD, NORFOLK
Water colour by Michael Angelo Rooker, 1743-1801

century and yet not forfeit the advantages of the hand labour and the thrift of our ancestors.'' This was written in the last century and the problem still remains to a large extent unsolved.

There is thus a sense in which perhaps this East Anglian farm-house might be preferred above its West Country fellow for all the latter's interesting array of contents. It is alive. History is still being made here, with every adaptation to new conditions, indoors or out, and every attempt of the inmates to "enjoy the intellectual progress of the century."

The change, I have said, is superficial: underneath, there is really not so very much to choose between this farm-house and any other of a similar size and fortune up and down the land. Something there is that unites them all, and for lack of a better word I must call it atmosphere. No change of fashion or attention to the calls of progress can obliterate this atmosphere, which continually reminds us, by its silence and flowery peace, of the surrounding fields upon which in the end every farm-house depends and from which it draws its essential character. In a farm-house only the thinnest of lines divides outdoors from in. When the men come in from the field they bring its mud with them; or from the orchard they bring an apple or

14

two in their pockets; and from the harvest field an ear of corn, extra heavy in the yield, to stick in the mirror over the mantel-piece. The doors of the old house are open and the rooms are full of air. A lowing of cows can be heard from one of the meadows across the way where they have crowded up to the gate, urgent in their demonstration that it is high time they were milked. A duck with a mended leg waddles across the kitchen floor, as much at home there as are the cat and dog. The farmer's gun, its steel side-locks etched with a picture of game-birds, is propped up against the wall behind the copper, ready for him to rush indoors and snatch it up as opportunity occurs—a covey of partridges in the stubble, maybe, or a rat in the yard.

The talk in the kitchen is all of stock and crop, and the farmer's wife knows as much about these things as she does about the topics with which women usually concern themselves. She must be ready at a moment's notice to give a hand with an ailing animal or to deal with a caller in her husband's absence. At harvest and haysel she must carry food and drink out to the men in the fields. Pig-killing time finds her making brawns and· sausages, or boiling up the lard, rosemary-flavoured, or curing hams after a recipe zealously guarded through generations. If she is a hill-farmer's wife she must be prepared to go up the fells and help to bring down the sheep for branding and shearing. And it is the ever-presentness of these activities that gives the farm-house its peculiar character, quite as much as the architecture of the building itself.

INTERIOR OF A FARM-HOUSE IN DENTDALE, YORKSHIRE
Water colour by Charles West Cope, 1811-1890

15

PRIORY FARM-HOUSE, BICESTER, OXFORDSHIRE
Water colour by Alfred Rimmer, 1829-1893

OF FARM-HOUSES ALL OVER THE COUNTRY

THE English rural scene owes much of its appeal to the unusually wide variety that is contained within its comparatively narrow compass. A single county will be productive of the most surprising opposites, whilst a journey from south to north, east to west, can be as scenically exciting to the observer as if he were journeying from one country to another. The granite villages behind the tip of Cornwall, bare as the back of your hand, could not well differ more than they do from the

16

A FARM-HOUSE IN SUSSEX
Unfinished water colour by William Henry Stothard Scott, 1783-1850

thatched and half-timbered villages of Essex, deployed so artlessly about their leafy greens; and a like dissimilarity characterises the villages of Cheshire and Norfolk, Sussex and Northumberland, Devon and Kent.

In the main, of course, this diversity of scenery is due to the nature of the geological structures upon which it is based. And this is true not only of plant-life, which finds in certain soils (and in certain soils only) the food necessary for its existence: it is also true of buildings, which, at any rate in former times, were mainly composed of material indigenous to the neighbourhood. It is largely the combination of these two factors, plant-life and building, trees and houses, that gives to a place its own peculiar character and scenic charm.

It is no part of my business in this short essay to prevent the smooth progress of the reader by intruding here a detailed geological survey of the country; yet I must hasten to add that, unless he is prepared to attempt the mastery of such a survey, he certainly cannot claim that his appreciation of the English scene is in any way complete. It is all very well to talk about the "smiling face" of England; but it should be borne in mind, in so doing, that the smile would not be there but for the bones across which it is stretched. Of these two contributing factors which together play so important a part in the determination of scenic character, plant-life is not our concern, whilst a glance at the geological map of England will reveal at once how varied and complex the architectural contribution must be.

Boldly ignoring the technical terms which have been fastened on to the several geological strata, we can perhaps gain a sufficient idea for our

OLD TILED BARNS AND FARMYARD
Water colour by George Price Boyce, 1883

immediate purpose if we translate the more outstanding of these terms into the names of the local building materials. Thus, granite, with slatey rock and some sandstone, occupies most of the western seaboard counties overlooking the Atlantic. Next, north to south, comes a predominantly sandstone area. This is followed by a belt of limestone which stretches across the country from Yorkshire in the north to Dorset in the south. Chalk and flint monopolise the next belt, from Hampshire and Berkshire to Norfolk, whilst Kentish rag fills in the extreme south-eastern corner. Admittedly this is an extremely rough-and-ready simplification of what is in fact a complex structure: nevertheless it should provide the reader with a sufficient clue as to why one type of building is to be found here and quite a different type there—granite houses in Cornwall or Cumberland, for instance, limestone in Somerset or Gloucestershire or Northamptonshire, half-timber in Essex, and flint in Norfolk.

"Wherever you spend your holiday," writes Mr. Arnold Fellows, in his informative *Wayfarer's Companion*, "you will find a local idiom in building, much as you do in dialect." It is an apt comparison. The old builders, in using the building material which was readiest to hand, not only employed what was most indigenously suitable to the locality but what was also (by use and long custom) most adaptable to their sense of

FARM BUILDINGS AT PRINCES RISBOROUGH, BUCKINGHAMSHIRE
Water colour by Samuel Palmer, 1805-1881

craftsmanship. Instinctively they knew exactly what to do with such material, how to make the best of it in every possible way, since, so to speak, the very feel of it was in their blood and they could not well go wrong. I suppose this is most of all obvious in the great limestone belt that runs across the country from Dorset to Yorkshire. Nowhere will you find a better architecture, for the simple reason that not only were the builders working in the material they best understood but the material itself was beautifully malleable to their purpose. There is no need, in the limestone country, to confine oneself to ecclesiastical architecture if one would see the best the district can offer: farm-houses and cottages provide, within their obvious limitations, quite as interesting a spectacle.

In a way, of course, the very handicaps which the material of certain localities imposed upon the builder were themselves a blessing in disguise. They constituted a discipline which, when overcome, resulted in an architecture of peculiar fitness. How exactly, for instance, the simple, austere lines of the granite architecture of the Lake District suits the rough, rocky landscape upon which it is built. The finials, the carved oriel windows, the ornamental drip-stones and porches and ridge-ends of the architecture of the limestone belt would here look out of place. And how admirably fitted to the spacious, wooded landscape of north-west Essex are its

FARM-HOUSE, SUTTON COLDFIELD, WARWICKSHIRE
Drawing by Charles Barber, 1806

half-timbered houses, containing, as they do, in their massive oaken beams, the durable relics of the huge forest that once covered the whole of the county and beyond. Stone, for all its beauty, would be unwelcome here for general use, as it would also be in Shropshire, whose "magpie" houses, illustrative of another idiomatic use of timber, so well become that county's leafy scene and rather fey, borderland spirit.

These instances show the appropriateness of the use of local building material in some of the larger and more obvious geological divisions of the country; but the smaller divisions are often no less suitably served. The flint building of Norfolk is a case in point. One would have supposed that, of all intractable and uncomely material for architectural use, this, surely, was the least likely to be productive of any sort of grace and beauty. Indeed, strangers, unaccustomed to the sight of flint walls, do sometimes find it an unattractive material. Closer acquaintance, however, usually modifies such an adverse opinion, whilst those who live with it, knowing it in all moods of the weather, shadow or shine, wet or dry, will readily attest to its most individual appeal. In certain lights the hard, uneven surfaces of the flints flash with points of fire; in others they smoulder as sullen as

20

EAST CLOTWORTHY FARM, NORTH DEVON
Drawing by C. F. Tunnicliffe, 1932

smoke; and rain discovers yet other hidden beauties. Colours innumerable hide in them, to be revealed only to the watchful and constant admirer. It is usual to set the flints between narrow brick courses, a builder's device which, though dictated by necessity, is not undecorative; and sometimes the blackest of the flints are themselves arranged in patterns (diamonds, lozenges, and so forth) to the additional charm of the building. Or again, to take one more example of a limited, local architecture, what could be more suitable to its surroundings than the use of weather-board in the deep estuaries of Essex and Suffolk? Already, before one comes within sight or smell of the sea, there are signs that betray its nearness, and of these not the least inspiriting is the use of weather-board for building. Presently the maze of oozy channels, sea-lavender-lined, begin to appear: it is the flat no-man's-land where pasture and water interlace, so that cows at graze and yachts at anchor seem equally expected. In such a scene what better building device could have been imagined than that which imitates the boats themselves?

So, all over the country, this "local idiom" in architecture reminds us of the virtue in that necessity which compelled the builders of long ago to look no further than their own immediate neighbourhood for the materials of their craft. It is so both with farm-houses and with cottages; but our immediate concern is with the former only.

A farm-house is more than merely a place to live in: it is a place for a farmer to live in, and, as such, it demands its own special design. Strictly speaking, it cannot usefully be considered apart from the farm-buildings of which it is the hub. More often than not, the farm-house and the out-buildings hang together in one pattern: a farm-stead comprises barns and byres, stables and stock-yard, as well as farm-house. And in the hey-day of farming, as may be seen in the plans and diagrams sprinkled over the pages of many a nineteenth-century book on agriculture, the whole stedding was conceived as a unit. Sometimes, however, the unity is achieved by casual addition rather than by planned forethought. In either case, the farm-house is only one section of the whole pile of buildings from the general arrangement of which it borrows no small part of its character. One side or more of the farmer's garden, for instance, will be bordered by the walls of his barns and granaries on which he grows his choicest plums and pears. It used to be considered an asset to an arable farm when, from any one spot on it, the master could view all his acres at a glance and so see what was going on in any field at any time. Similarly, to have all the buildings in one compact cluster is an equal advantage, since all is then at hand.

Such a compact grouping of farm-buildings is perhaps commonest in the north, as might be expected, where the weather is severe and where there are often great distances between one farm and the next. Northumberland and Durham possibly provide the best examples, the buildings usually being set around a closed court-yard. The almost feudal effect of such a grouping is further emphasised by the substantial nature of the structure of the buildings: from house to stable, cart-shed to byre, all is made to endure and to withstand. The proportions too are large, as becomes counties of so rich an agriculture. Not a few of the farms bear the imprint of the early nineteenth century—those generous days of High Farming when architects were encouraged to design farm-steads that should be worthy of the many agricultural developments of the time. The general effect of the Northumbrian "local idiom," however, remains one of severity, dictated as much by the use of stone as by the obvious necessity for strength; but this severity is sometimes nicely relieved by the judicious use of wide, sweeping arches, with decorative keystones, and by a certain solid comeliness of the whole group.

Much the same pattern holds in Cumberland and the Lake District in general; but here the severity is even increased by the use of granite and by a much more primitive architecture. I know that the farm-houses of the north-west are often colour-washed, and very effective they look scattered like shorn sheep over the distant green hillsides. All the same, my accusation of severity must hold—at least on a nearer view. Hill farming

LEE FARM, EAST CHESHIRE
Water colour by C. F. Tunnicliffe, 1928

is hard work with scant returns for it; and this fact, together with a certain dourness and frugality in the people, is reflected in many of the old farmsteads of the Lakes. But if life is hard there and somewhat lacking in grace, it has its very real compensations. Such a spare livelihood must be eked out, if possible, with catering for summer visitors; and many a southerner, shy at first as he enters the dark building, grimly shadowed by the hills, has come at last to experience an affection for the stark simplicity of the place and for the warm-hearted responses of those who live there. I have in mind at the moment an old farm-house on the hillside overlooking Loweswater. ("Overlooking" is perhaps the wrong word, since this farm-house, following the usual custom here, turned its back on the magnificent view up the Lake, with Crummock Water and Buttermere beyond and all the encircling hills, and faced on to the midden in the court-yard. "There's no money in views," I was told, when I deplored this fact.) The lay-out of this particular farm-house was typical. A long, tree-lined approach, between deep banks full of violets in the Spring, brought one immediately into the midst of the barns and out-buildings, and not, as one might have expected, to the farm-house. Tucked in among these buildings was the

23

hind's house (somewhat the equivalent of a bailiff) as if it were his duty to guard the approach and be most immediately on the spot in case of necessity. His house was little more than a cottage. The lane then circled the cluster of farm-buildings and entered directly into the great court-yard.

It was April when I was there, and a bright sun sparkled on the water; but in that enclosed court-yard, surrounded by the stern, forbidding granite barns and the no less forbidding farm-house, a wintry chill asserted itself and the last thing one had in mind was the shining lakes and the wild daffodils that grow beside them. Comfort, as the sybarite seeks it, is sin to the strong-hearted northener of the hills; and there was certainly little enough of it in this old farm-house, with its cold, flagged floors, its stout, darkened beams, and its spare, simple furniture. It was twilight at mid-day here—a twilight that hardly allowed one to see the muslin-wrapped hams hanging from the ceiling or the family portraits on the walls. Yet, as I sat eating the meal so generously provided for me and talked with the farmer's old mother as she sat by the kitchen range—her feet lifted off the flagged floor by a hassock, her work-and-age-shrunken hands folded on her lap— I thought I caught more than a glimpse of such a nutty character as sugges-ted there might be truth after all in the contention that, although the hill farmer may live near to the bone, his life is sometimes the sweeter for it.

Perhaps it is the East Anglian in me that finds in granite a grimness as well as a strength. At any rate, whether it be in the hard North or the soft South, granite, as a building material, does not appeal much to me. If I do not like it in Cumberland, for instance, where every rain-bearing hill proclaims its fitness, how should I like it in Cornwall, where the warm sun brings the first flowers to our island? Indeed, I could sometimes fancy, by the look of some of the old farm-steads there, that the builders did not like it much, either. Eaveless roofs, small windows, straight lines everywhere— the buildings never seem to triumph over the sheer intractability of the material in which they are fashioned. Nor does the general bareness of the landscape help matters much: except in the valleys no trees relieve the austerity of the architecture with the wild, subtle rhythms of nature.

As different from these unrelenting stone houses of Cornwall as if they stood in another country and were inhabited by another race of people are the half-timbered farm-houses of the Welsh Border counties—Shropshire and Herefordshire, for instance, home of some of the finest master-builders this island has bred. All is grace here, the craftsman's delight in his material, the builder's relish of the "sweet, especial rural scene" with which it is his problem to co-operate and, by so doing, to adorn. "Magpie" building is the popular term for this particular kind of half-timbered dwelling, and indeed it is apt for the playful (even exuberant) weave of black beams on a clear white surface. Such master craftsmen as John Abel were the geniuses of this local Tudor fashion: they were, in fact, just as cunning in the employment of timber as their anonymous fellow-craftsmen of the

24

HANGLETON MANOR FARM, NEAR BRIGHTON

Oil painting by J. Morgan Rendle, 1945

FARM-HOUSE AND COTTAGES AT HATHERSAGE IN DERBYSHIRE

Painting in tempera by Harry E. Allen, 1947

oolite belt were in the employment of stone. John Abel came from Herefordshire and his best-known work was in the construction of larger houses and public buildings; but he was obviously a potent influence all over the Border counties and the infection of his genius is to be seen in farm-house and cottage. Incidentally, it has always seemed to me a pity that more of these great men, to whose skill we owe so much of our pleasure as we go about from county to county, are not recorded and remembered. I find a special pleasure when I come across such a tablet as that on the brick tower of Toppesfield church, in Essex, commemorating the sixteenth-century builder who was responsible. For the most part we do not even know the names of these benefactors, so prodigal of good workmanship was their age and so easily was their mastery taken for granted.

If the early half-timber farm-houses of East Anglia are less spectacular (at least from the outside) that is partly because, more often than not, the wood is entirely hidden from view beneath a coat of plaster. To see the beams of these grand old farm-houses one must go indoors. Only here and there does one see a house with its beams exposed; and though the effect then may be delightful and evocative of a quick response from the passerby, it is a mistake thus to seek to win such easy admiration—as the occupants have probably discovered. The builders of these houses knew what they were doing when they gave the wooden framework a substantial filling of wattle and daub, than which they could hardly have contrived a better non-conductor. Nowhere can be colder and windier than East Anglia in the forefront of the year when the West Country is already beginning to show its first buds and green leaf-tips; and the best place to be at such a time is behind the well-packed walls of a half-timber house that has stood the weather of four or more hundred years.

Mostly the larger farm-houses of East Anglia (and, whatever the regional partisans may say, I intend to include at least the north of Essex under this head) are built on the H pattern; that is to say, there are three blocks, of which the connecting block may originally have been (and sometimes still is) a one-storied hall. This part of the country abounded, formerly, in the yeoman class, countrymen whose like, for industry, integrity, a simple culture and a general worthiness, has never been equalled in this land; and a considerable number of the farm-houses here still bear witness to the dignified and responsible prosperity of this most excellent breed of men. Ample in proportion, without ostentation, and comely in design, these farm-houses represent one of the peaks of domestic architecture and are a standing witness to the good taste of their Tudor agrarian owners. Their plain exterior is often relieved with some admirable carving, particularly of the mouldings and brackets (bearing, it may be, the monogram of the owner) and barge-boarding. Sometimes, too, the whole face of the plaster is pargeted—though more often only a few isolated panels of this ingenious bas-relief remain to-day to remind us of the splendour that has

A MODERN FARMYARD AT POYNINGS, SUSSEX
Oil painting by J. Morgan Rendle, 1943

been. Pargeting, which varies from elaborate floral and bird design to the simple and traditional scallop pattern (said to have originated in an inspiration derived from the scallop-shell badge of returning Crusaders), is, like so much old architectural ornamentation, utilitarian in origin, its purpose being, of course, to break the fall of the rain as it runs down the walls and so save the plaster from disintegrating.

A word about the plaster itself may not be without interest, since this, in common with much other building material, has deteriorated in quality with the advent of newer and quicker and cheaper methods of manufacture. An old Essex man once described to me the method adopted by his father, who was a builder. He himself, as a boy, had had a hand in the job, earning, in the process, many a stern word of reprimand and "a clip on the ear," as he said, this being the way of instruction in those days. Cow-hair was bought at the local tannery, by the hundredweight, and this had first to be cleaned of dirt and teased so fine that, as my informant said, "it all fluffed up like thistledown." Short sticks, called "grubbers," were used

OAKRIDGE FARM, GLOUCESTERSHIRE, LATE SUMMER
Oil painting by Sir William Rothenstein, 1872-1945

for this purpose, the men (or boys) kneeling on the ground round the heap of matted hair and beating it as if they were tapping out a tune with a couple of drum-sticks. A ring of lime was then made, with an outer ring of sand, and in the centre the fluffed-up hair was placed. This latter was then damped and the whole tirelessly mixed together, and the master-builder would pass no plaster that did not meet with his expert approval. "Instead of wasting away," said the old man, "like plaster does nowadays, that only got harder and better as the years went by"—in proof of which it is only necessary to examine some portion of old plaster from the brick-work of an ancient house.

One feature of the finest of these old yeoman farm-houses never fails to attract attention. I mean the chimney-stack. Often this consists of a cluster of chimneys based upon a central flue, and the ornamentation is surprisingly beautiful. Each chimney of the cluster may be patterned differently, the favourite being a spiral; and the effect is to proclaim that here is a noble house, nobly fashioned and finished, a home, in a word, whose focus is

27

the great wood-filled hearth. Mainly, East Anglian farm-houses (unlike the cottages) are no longer thatched but tiled, and here nature has sometimes added a touch of poetry to the general appearance by the application of minute bosses of lichen, old gold or emerald green, which give as it were a patina to the tiled surface and can in certain lights be most attractive.

But the glory of these old houses, after all, is their timber—studs and beams and foot-polished floor-boards. It could have been no easy task to prepare the wood for a timber-framed house at the builder's yard, sorting it out according to its suitability, transporting it to the site and there erecting it, timber by timber, as had been planned. It happens that my own home is timber-framed, and several of the massive joints are marked with crudely chiselled roman figures, reminding me each time I see them of the builder's complex task; for there is no doubt that, after he had sorted out the timber at his yard, this for beams, that for joists, and so on, he numbered them so as to facilitate the final erection of the building on the site. All the timber-work, too, is secured with wooden pegs—not a nail anywhere; and the marks of the adze are clearly visible. Sometimes, no doubt, the wood (little but oak was used for these houses) came straight from the forest, of which to-day Epping is only a small remaining portion; but sometimes, also, it came from the ship-yards down on the coast, where the Tudor fleets were then being broken up. There are many timbers in my house which, by their shape, I like to suppose were originally ship's timbers, brought up from the coast on horse-drawn waggons and given by the builder a new lease of life. Hard as iron, they have withstood the centuries and are good for many centuries yet to come. One of the besetting dangers of such old timber-framed houses is that they often become riddled with worm and beetle, so that parts of the beams will crumble away to dust. Valuable research has been done in the matter however, of recent years, and it is now possible to arrest this form of decay permanently, leaving a hard core of wood that will outlast many of the buildings of to-day.

Different again from these East Anglian farm-houses are those of East Sussex and the Weald of Kent. These, especially in such places as Goudhurst, Biddenden and all the rest of the "dens," are indeed of rare beauty, as appealing in colour as comely in design. Just as I personally like the combination, in brick nogging, of black wood and red brick, so too I like the combination in Kent and Sussex of hanging tiles, red as any Tudor wall in a sunny garden, and tarred weather-board—though I admit that it is more usual for the latter to be painted white. Those hanging, rosy tiles are the chief characteristic of the architecture of this region: they seem to add warmth to what are anyway two of the warmer counties. (Incidentally, tile-hung walls are one of the oldest architectural devices. It was common in Saxon times for both walls and roof to be tile-hung, only then the tiles were wooden shingles, such as may be seen to-day on some church spires. The intention, of course, was to secure a waterproof surface. Tile-hanging

KENTISH FARM BUILDINGS WITH OLD OAST-HOUSE
Water colour by Rowland Hilder, 1944

is a feature in Surrey, as well as in Sussex and Kent; and slates are used
in a similar way in the north-west, also in Devon and Cornwall.) Another
feature of the Sussex and Kent farm-house architecture is the steep angle
of the roof, so designed that the contained attics of the third storey are
almost as spacious as the rooms on the first. Surrounded by their various
out-buildings, these old farm-houses are as inviting, as slumbrous and sun-
loving as any in the land; and a happy focus is usually given to the confused
pile by the round oast-house, with its white-fingered cowl (where this has
not been removed, as is too often the case in Sussex, leaving a blunt-tipped,
ugly kiln) conveniently pointing the direction of the prevailing wind.

Apart from design and ornamentation, much of the charm of a house
depends upon the nature of the material of which it is constructed and
upon the reactions of this material to the continually changing play of
light in our unpredictable climate. Plaster, for instance, to be seen at its
best, needs the burning concentration of strong sunlight (which, incidentally, is one of the reasons why it is so apt for sunny East Anglia). No wall
surface, however cunningly decorated by the craftsman's skill, can match
the plain white plaster wall of a house across which falls the shadow-
tracery of wintered boughs. The red, hung tiles of Sussex seem actually
designed to fit into the warm landscape of the south. And what better
building material could possibly have been devised for the Cotswolds,

29

whose high, open contours take the sun like an outstretched hand, than the light-absorbing oolite? The texture seems to change, not only with the locality, but with every mood of the day and the weather. It is one of the paradoxes of this attractive architecture that, although the material is so strong and durable, the effect is of softness, even tenderness, of outline. Sharp edges and spare lines cannot lessen the sensuousness of a total effect to which shadow and shine are equally contributive.

And brick, old brick, will assert its charm wherever it be found, whether in the Home Counties and the Midlands, where it most abounds, or, more sparsely, elsewhere. Those who are familiar with brick only as it is to be seen in modern houses, raw in colour and too bulky in design, can have no idea how lovely a seventeenth- or eighteenth-century brick house can be. Weathering, of course, has something to do with it: nothing is more gracious, in the way of building material, than old brick walls that have mellowed with hundreds of years of sun and rain and whose surface has been crumbled by wind's tooth and wasp's. But weathering is not the only cause of charm in old brick buildings. The size of early bricks is a contributor: they were a good deal thinner. And more important still is the way they were laid. Before Queen Anne, bonding (as it is called) was done in alternate rows of "headers" and "stretchers," that is one row all ends and the next row all sides. Besides strengthening the walls, this method avoided a too uniformly patterned surface. It is called the English bond. In the eighteenth century, a different method was introduced, called the Flemish bond, in which headers and stretchers were used alternately in the same row, thus breaking up the surface even more. Incidentally, these two methods of bonding old bricks provide a rough clue to the dating of the house.

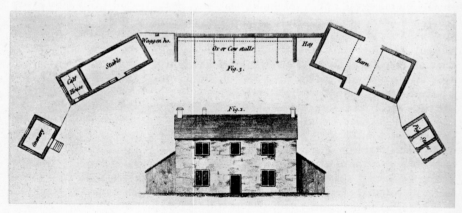

MIXED FARM AND OFFICES
Engraving from R. W. Dickson's *Practical Agriculture*, 1805

DALE FARM, YORKSHIRE
Water colour by Grace Gabler, 1944

But to the appeal of the texture of the stone itself, in the Cotswolds, must be added the appeal of manifold decoration: no material could have been more amenable to the genius of the mediæval builder, it seems, than Cotswold oolite. From the gable-ends, like those stack ornaments with which the thatcher displays his skill and ingenuity in the use of straw, finials were attached with as much play of the imagination as if the builder were at work on a church rather than a farm-house. Every window has its carefully proportioned drip-stones, as delightful an addition to the general æsthetic effect as they are useful in helping to keep the rain off the glass. Doorways really do invite, as doorways should, if not always with the extension of a decorated porch, complete with side-seats wherefrom to watch the world go by (or just the sun setting over the hills), then at least with welcoming arch. Even the building-stone, so squarely cut and evenly set, is relieved by the necessary imposition of larger, strengthening stones at the quoins.

These ornamentations and decorations by no means complete the list, so free a rein did limestone allow to the hand of the builder and so responsive was it to his fancy. The squarely built chimney-stacks, else quite austere, are relieved by the simple addition of coping and drip-moulding, whilst the roof, covered with the native stone slates, cunningly exploits both perspective and utility by a method of laying the slates in diminishing sizes from eaves to ridge. Of these slates a whole book might be written, from quarrying to building, so rich are they in the lore and practice of craftsmanship. "In the west of England," writes Mr. James Kenward, in his admirable book *The Roof Tree*, "where stone slates are used, the heaviest stones are laid next above the eaves so that the walls take the weight of them; above these are laid the next in weight, and so on, to the lightest laid at the ridge. The slaters had to give each weight and thickness a name, so that they could call down for them, and the names they gave were as lovely and comic as the country names of wild flowers. Batchelors, Farewells, Short Backs and Long Backs, Shorts Save One, Jenny Why Gettest Thou, Rogue Why Winkest Thou . . ."

A house, constructed out of local material and designed in the local tradition, will inevitably seem to grow out of the landscape enfolding it; and if this is perhaps nowhere quite so obvious as in the Cotswolds and in Yorkshire—and indeed in the limestone belt altogether—it is, essentially, just as true elsewhere, in West Sussex, for instance, and in Berkshire. It is true of all the building materials I have already mentioned; and to these, others should be added which are no less indigenous and which contribute to the astonishing variety of this island's homelier architecture. In Devon, for example, one of the commonest building materials is cobb, a mixing of clay with straw. The method of building with cobb in Devon (and in that part of the neighbouring county of Somerset which lies outside the limestone belt) is nicely indicative of the more leisurely way in which our forefathers were able to set about their jobs. The mixture of clay and straw is put on (or I should say was put on) a layer, or "raise," at a time, each layer being allowed to dry before the next is added, so that as much as two years may be required in building a house. The result, however, was worth it. In fact, the only drawback of cobb is that, if not properly protected, it disintegrates with the damp, and so it is usual to set the walls on a tarred plinth (or perhaps on stone) and to protect them above with a deep overhang of thatch. There used to be an old Devon saying to the effect that all cobb needed was a good hat and a stout pair of boots. Another feature of cobb building is the rounded corners which may have originated in an attempt to overcome a tendency to crack, and the attractive colour-wash that is often employed to decorate the walls. Cobb for clayey Devon; but what about the chalk-lands, such as Buckinghamshire? Once again, the local material is pressed into service and the result is wichert, in other words, chalk mud mixed with chopped straw. But whether it be cobb or wichert, clunch (a durable form of chalk used in Sussex) or plaster, there is no denying the fitness of such building material for the locality in which it is found: it "belongs."

WILLY LOTT'S HOUSE AT EAST BERGHOLT, SUFFOLK

Oil sketch by John Constable, 1776–1837
In the Christchurch Mansion Collection

THE BEEKEEPER

Oil painting by Gilbert Spencer, 1947

OF COTTAGES IN GENERAL

COTTAGES have this at least in common with farm-houses, that for the most part the material of which they are built is dictated by the local geology: stone cottages, whether thatched or tiled, in the limestone belt, granite in the south and west, timber and plaster in the east, and so on. Or at any rate, that is how it used to be. To-day we have entered upon the age of standardisation; and individuality in cottage architecture is becoming as obsolete as individuality in the clothes and manners and amusements of the cottagers themselves. Only in the remoter parts, away from the towns, away even from the villages, may we presently expect to find those characteristic cottages which, for all their inconveniences, had anyway the merit of aptness to the local scene. I admit that in the main the cottager seems to prefer the new, standardised Rural District Council cottages and does not rail against the rules and regulations with which he finds himself beset when he moves into them. They have amenities, they are on the 'bus route, they are roomy; and it is apparently old-fashioned to expect a cottager, whose garden used to mean so much to him, to resent the lack of privacy and deplore the fact (for instance) that he may not nail a creeper to his wall or plant anything taller than a gooseberry bush. "I never did live within sight of anybody else's chimney," I remember an old countryman saying, when, for the sake of convenience, his children tried to persuade him to live with them nearer the town, "and I hope I never shall." But the new generation holds otherwise.

By one of her more enlightened statutes, Queen Elizabeth ordered that four acres of land should be attached to each cottage let to agricultural labourers. This was the beginning, or perhaps I should say the consolidation, of that era of freeholders and copyholders who, out of their modest prosperity, built for themselves those decent cottage homes of which many, survive in England to-day and of which there would be many more if Enclosure had not, by laying land to land, transformed a contented and largely self-supporting cottage population into one of dispossessed labourers. In a word, it is the cottages of the sixteenth and seventeenth centuries we mainly have in mind when we speak of traditional English cottage architecture. Previous to this the labourer's cottage had been little better than a mud hut, consisting of one room only and conducive to the lowest possible standards of domestic life. As for subsequent cottages, these, like the larger houses of the period, were more solid than beautiful: nothing in architecture is more depressing than the four-square brick cottage of the nineteenth century put up by a local builder in whom every vestige of good craftsmanship had disappeared. All trace of the early mud hovels has long since vanished and any account of our cottage architecture had best begin with those simple, timber-framed and stone or brick erections with which, in varying degrees of alteration and addition, we are still familiar.

COTTAGES IN THE NEW FOREST
Drawing by John Constable, 1820

No doubt in their original state these early cottages were, by modern standards, exceedingly comfortless: cold, draughty, full of smoke, inconvenient. They were, nevertheless, a great improvement upon their predecessors; and indeed it is a matter for no small astonishment that cottage architecture should, in a comparatively short while, have achieved even such a degree of solidity and comfort. Once the basic plan had been realised, it was not long before improvements were added, and many of the cottages built during this period (and especially towards the end of the seventeenth century) are as sturdy and secure to-day as when they were built.

The plan of a typical cottage of, say, the seventeenth century reveals a very simple design. The ground floor consists of one main room, with open hearth (including bread-oven) and staircase, and one smaller room (sometimes called the "back-'us") without any fireplace. These rooms vary surprisingly little in size and the measurements of the whole structure (at least in timber-framed cottages) are usually about twenty-two or twenty-three feet long by sixteen feet wide. Overhead there are two bedrooms, into one of which the staircase directly opens, productive of a continuous draught unless provided with a trap-door. These rooms also are fireless. The advantage of a central chimney-stack is therefore obvious: it will at

34

OLD COTTAGE
Drawing by John Crome, 1768-1821

least do something to help raise the temperature of the three unheated rooms.

A special word may be said about the open hearth, since this is, after all, the centre and focus of the whole cottage. Six to seven feet is the usual width, the depth being about half this. A seat is let into the wall on one side, and on the other is the door of the bread-oven. Perhaps the cottager of those earlier days was more immune to smoke than we are, for most of us who possess such open hearths now find it essential to install a suspended "hood" of some sort that will canalise the draught. The open hearth was intended, of course, solely for the burning of wood; and when it is remembered with what rapidity such a hearth will burn up a ton of logs, it will be understood that an enormous amount of the country's timber must have been used up in its cottage fires. Whatever its disadvantages, the open hearth had at least this considerable advantage for the Hodge of those days, who had to be up earlier in the morning than his successor to-day, that it never really went out. The ashes were raked over in the morning, a little kindling was laid on, and, with the aid of the bellows (or the cottager's own breath), a blaze was soon started. "An old man living on the hills at Hyde Heath," writes Mr. G. Eland, in his scholarly

35

OLD COTTAGE, WITH FOUR-BARRED GATE
Wash drawing by John Crome, 1768-1821

little book, *In Bucks*, "told the writer that he always kept a store of dried cow-droppings, and that one of them placed on the embers in the morning and blown with the bellows soon provided an excellent means of grilling a rasher of bacon, which was laid upon it."

The earliest floors, for the downstairs rooms, were of earth, spread with rushes. It was not until much later that bricks, in the timber areas, and flag-stones, in the stone areas, were used, to be sprinkled, this time, with sand. (Old people in my own village will tell how a man used to come round every Saturday morning, with a couple of donkeys, delivering sand. They would buy a quart at a time: "and very nice it looked, too, the yellow sand on the clean, red bricks.") But if the downstairs floor was earthen, upstairs it was board-and-joist. The wide boards, oak or elm, smooth with much treading, are a feature of many an old cottage still. They are also the despair of the modern housewife, who likes to see her furniture standing straight and without the aid of blocks of wood under its legs; for they will tilt at quite extraordinary angles where the framework has, as we say, "settled" on its clay foundations.

Originally the window had indeed been the wind-eye, or, more strictly speaking, the wind-hole, an aperture through which the cottager might see what was going on outside. From this it developed into a shuttered

A COTTAGE SCENE
Water colour by Kate Greenaway, 1846-1901

hole and thence into a framed hole—but still a wind-hole. Some attempt
to keep the wind out was introduced with the use of a lattice of wattles.
Horn next filled the lattice, then glass. Later still, the lattice ceased to be
made of wood and was hammered out of lead, as may be seen even to-day.
Lead-glazing was a minor rural craft until comparatively recently: its
practitioner ranged the countryside, travelling many miles in the course of
the day, with his sheets of glass slung over his back in a frame and the rest
of his stock-in-trade dangling beneath it. Where such windows still exist
in cottages they are often beautified with wrought-iron catches of fine
craftsmanship; but these were later additions, usually of the early nineteenth
century, the hey-day of the English blacksmith as of many other craftsmen.
The earliest windows did not open on a hinge but slid along in a groove.
Many examples of such windows still exist. Incidentally, in Essex they
were placed high in the wall, immediately under the ceiling.

And, as windows were in fact wind-eyes, so staircases were in fact cases
(or cupboards) built round the stairs. But the staircase, opening from a
little bobbined door beside the fireplace, was an eighteenth (or more
probably nineteenth) century addition. Its predecessor was a ladder; and
it would throw an interesting light on the workings of the builder's and
craftsman's mind if we could study the evolution of that ladder, through

37

the notched piece of timber, to the enclosed flight of stairs with its "treads," its "strings" and its "risers." If the stairs had a cupboard, however, that was about the only cupboard these old cottages could boast. The simple four-square plan admitted of no such aids to domesticity and Hodge's wife must have had her work cut out to keep away the flies and dust, if she bothered about such things. Those corner cupboards, which now command fancy prices at the sales, were an outright necessity then and it was a much later development to rip their doors off and use them for the display of china and ornaments. Equally necessary in those days was the chest, for linen and clothes. As this was often handed on from generation to generation, like the bed, it was not only strong and well-made, of chosen oak, but also, not infrequently, carved on the front panels. Of different kind and later date was the bread-trough, in which the family's bread was mixed and the flour kept safe and dry. Examples of these old troughs are still fairly common, especially in East Anglia, where they are called "trows" and are set on splayed legs and ornamented, more often than not, with a carved skirting. To-day, it is true, they are mostly to be found relegated to the shed at the back of the cottage, where they provide a handy receptacle for hens' food.

The traditional roofing for a timber-framed cottage was thatch. Of recent years a prejudice has grown up against the use of thatch, not un-influenced perhaps by the difficulty of getting it replaced these days and by the frowning attitude of the insurance companies. It is claimed that thatch is too exposed to destruction by fire and that in any case it soon falls to pieces. Sparks from a passing traction-engine, in dry weather, might certainly set a thatch on fire; but how often nowadays does one see a traction-engine on the roads? There have been instances, of course, as at Olney, where, in the days of universal thatch, whole streets were destroyed by fire; and even to-day one may come upon examples of the long-poled iron hooks (as at Thaxted Guildhall) which were used to rake off the burning thatch and so prevent the fire from spreading. A more considerable difficulty now, however, is to find a thatcher, since, in common with so many rural crafts, apprentices are hard to come by. As for the claim that thatch soon falls to pieces and is very expensive to replace, this is to a certain extent true; but why let it fall to pieces? Wind will work a lot of damage in a thatch, once it gets under the ridge and eaves, and sparrows and starlings, by burrowing into it and pulling out the straws, can soon cause considerable harm; but both these evils can, to a large extent, be mitigated by a covering of wire-netting. Indeed, I would not exchange thatch for any other form of roofing, since it is not only good to look at but is also warm in winter and cool in summer.

Incidentally, there are quite a number of different materials used for thatching, even now, up and down the countryside. Most people are familiar with two only: straw and reed. But the late Thomas Hennell, who knew

HEARING LESSONS: A COTTAGE INTERIOR
Water colour by William Henry Hunt, 1790-1864

most of what was to be known about such country matters, enumerated
several other thatching materials from various parts of the country. "In
Norfolk river-reed, in Essex rushes, in Dorset reed made from wheat-
straw, in parts of Somerset rye-straw, which is grown solely for this
purpose and cut green; in most other places wheat- or oat-straw from the
threshing-machine, on moors and mountains furze, heather or bracken."
Nor is even this list complete, and Mr. Hennell himself gives two more
unusual materials: the stems of flax that had been grown for linseed and
cut with the reaping-machine, from Suffolk, and shavings gathered from
the local coopers' yards, from near Petworth, in Sussex.

39

Since it is very rare indeed for a cottage to be built to-day with a thatched roof, there is not often an opportunity for watching the whole process. The most we usually see is a new "coat" being imposed on an old "waistcoat": but let me first explain these appropriate terms. The waistcoat is the first thatch and is attached directly on to the rafters of the cottage, sewn on, in fact, with an enormous needle threaded with tarred rope. Two men work on this part of the job, one outside the roof and the other underneath, each passing the needle through the straw to the other. This waistcoat is about a foot thick. What we often see being renewed is the coat, which is fastened on to the waistcoat by means of spicks or spars, i.e. double-twisted lengths of green hazel or sallow, shaped like hair-pins. Strips of split wood, called "ledgers," are secured as further support at such vulnerable places as ridge or eaves, and, just to make doubly sure, these are sometimes arranged attractively in diamond pattern. The trickiest parts of a thatch are round the dormer windows, if any, for here, if the straw is not arranged so that the rain can easily run off, rot may set in at the hollows. All told, thatching provides as good an example as any of the axiom, applicable to most crafts, that use is the foundation of much of the best traditional ornament. Every one of the thatcher's ornamental devices, though they may attract attention to-day mainly for their "quaint-ness" and though the thatcher himself may be (and mostly is) ignorant of their first purpose, had their origin in utility.

Many changes and developments were made in the English cottage during the nineteenth century, and it has been left to the invading towns-man of to-day to strip away the improvements (or otherwise) and reveal the original shell. With the increase in the means of communication and the consequently wider and cheaper use of coal, for instance, most open hearths were filled in and replaced by a kitchen stove, with a small oven on one or both sides. The remainder of the space was often utilised for the insertion of a cupboard, which, being set close against the fire, was free of the common cottage curse of dampness. The staircase did not admit of much improvement, for the simple reason that there was no room; and so the narrow treads continued to make ascent and descent an extremely perilous adventure, undertaken, more often than not, crabwise. If lattice windows remained, rattling with every wind, they were few and far between: for the most part they were removed to make way for hinged or sash-windows. Only their size remained unchanged, though small windows in a cottage may matter less than the anxious improver supposes, seeing that even such light as they might admit is usually denied by the pots of geraniums and other window-flowers in which the cottager delights.

The spartan inhabitants of those earlier cottages would, furthermore, be amazed at the quantity and quality of the furniture which, during the nineteenth century, had become the accepted and necessary property of the humblest cottager. Some of this furniture was indeed of excellent

AUTUMN 1946 : COTTAGES AT GREAT BARDFIELD IN ESSEX

Oil painting by John Aldridge

THE GIRL AT THE GATE

Oil painting by Sir George Clausen, 1889

craftsmanship. Those old windsor chairs and arm-chairs may only have been turned out on a pole-lathe by some bodger in the deep heart of a beechwood; but for all that they were as good to look at as they were durable, as comfortable as they were conformable. Mostly they were made entirely of beechwood, but sometimes the seats were of oak. Cherry was also used occasionally, good in grain and sweet to smell; and rarer still were the yew chairs. Those round tables on well-turned tripod legs, though they may have had their origin in the necessity to make the most of a little space, were every one a compliment both to the skill of their rural makers and to the innate good taste (unspoiled as yet by the imposition of mass-produced and mass-designed articles) of their owners. The quantity and quality of the utensils, also, would have amazed the early cottager, not to mention the display of ornaments—a couple of glazed dogs on the mantelpiece, a Staffordshire figure here and a Newcastle bowl there, sent home by a sailor son as his farewell gift, a harvest mug or a lustre jug. All these things, spurned by the cottager of to-day and salvaged by the collector, added a pleasant note of colour and unforced gaiety to the cottage interior and revealed an immense advance, in a comparatively short while, upon the comfortless furniture and heavy platters, the general sense of domestic austerity, of an earlier age.

But most, I fancy, that seventeenth-century cottager would have been struck by the improvements in the gardens. Gradually, through generations, the cottager has evolved a whole horticulture of his own. Use, though this still comes first and foremost, is no longer the sole criterion of what he shall grow in that little patch of land which he may have to quit to-morrow and which is the nearest he has ever come to the ownership of the soil which it has been his life's care to tend. His vegetables, immensely increased in variety and improved in quality during the last century, provide no mean addition to his larder. His fruit trees, plum and damson, apple and pear, are his joy—he knows their history from pip onwards and their yield is his continuous theme. Even his hedges and paths betray the excellent husbandry which, through depressed and despised generations, he has inherited from his fathers. Then there are his flowers. These, unless it be his roses, are, it is true, usually the affair of his womenfolk and are mainly confined to the old-fashioned and fragrant sorts, pinks and lilies, daffodils and snowdrops, which more or less look after themselves. Conservative in all matters relating to the countryside, he is no lover of new species of flowers and fruit and can see nothing in ornamental shrubs. Herbs, however, though he has now forgotten their uses, are still a feature of his garden—rosemary, a bush of southernwood to snatch at and smell by the door, lavender along the path, and a clump of sage down at the end of the garden. English cottage gardens, in fact, are among the most attractive features of the rural scene, and in nothing are their owners so quick to show a very proper pride.

41

OF A VERY PARTICULAR COTTAGE

MOST of us, even if we are townsmen, respond readily enough to the prospect of a pleasing old cottage, though the chances are that we should not ourselves care to live in one. Perhaps it is a case of inherited memory. At the most we are rarely townsmen of more than a few generations' standing; and it may be that when we look at some especially attractive old cottage, with its flower-patch and leaning apple tree, something in us remembers the time when those of our own blood lived in a like place. "The best of us," wrote Richard Jefferies, "are polished cottagers." And if we have since forgotten the simple economy, the special technique—in short, the discipline—which cottage life demanded, at least we still remember the savour these things imparted—like the savour of summer fruit remembered in wintertime. And it is of this I wish to write now, the very spirit of English cottage life.

It happens that just before I sat down to write these words I was witness to a simple cottage scene which seems to me now to have had in it something of the savour I am trying to describe. The husband, an old man who in any other calling would by now have been put on the retired list but who, since he "went on the land" when he was a slip of a boy, must remain there (and would not have it otherwise) till he can no longer drag his limbs up the road to the farm, had just come in from the fields and was washing in a tin bowl under the apple tree outside his back door. He had turned his neck-band in, and in the leather belt round his waist was tucked a towel. As he splashed the water over his face the evening sun made diamonds of the falling drops. Then, rubbing himself with the towel, he turned towards me and I could see where the sunburn, year after year of it, weathered indelibly into the skin, ended in a straight line across his clear forehead. "Hard old water, that is," he said: "give me spring water any day of the week." At this, his wife, who was sitting in the doorway, joined in with reminiscences of the various springs in the locality, which were once the only source of supply and the differing merits of which she had known as a connoisseur knows his wines. "Best of all," she said, her eyes gazing beyond the hen- and faggot-filled back-yard to the far-off days when she was a girl in this same locality, "best of all was the spring up along the medders to Broadoaks. That laid on a stone bottom and was as clear as the air itself; and a wonderful drop o' tea that made. But this stuff—I don't know what they do put into it, I'm sure. You can smell it round the top of the kettle, many's the time." I suggested that anyway there were certain advantages, especially in a droughty season, in having "the Company's water" laid on to your door. "That's true enough," she replied, as she slowly pulled herself up from her chair and went into the kitchen to prepare the evening meal; but it was easy to see that she set little enough store by advantages won at the expense of a "wonderful

A DEVONSHIRE COTTAGE
Water colour by Francis Stevens, 1806

drop o' tea." It counted for nothing now, though it probably occasioned plenty of grumbling at the time, that before the pipes were laid this way every bucket of water had had to be fetched from a good quarter of a mile away, perhaps after a long day's work, or that, in dry seasons, the daily trek had led even further afield and often to ponds and ditches from which the green scum had first to be cleared away. "That never harmed we," she would probably have said, as one of her neighbours once proudly declared to me.

Or perhaps this spirit of English cottage life will reveal itself, unexpectedly and in a flash, to the sensitive passer-by. It is a warm spring day, for instance, with clouds of plum blossom a-dazzle under blue skies; and beneath the fruit trees in the narrow garden a woman bends over her washing, which the good morning (and the gloom of the tiny lean-to in which so much of her day must be spent) has compelled her to do outdoors. She looks the proper subject for a Clausen to paint. . . . Or again: it is high summer this time. The long evening scarcely increases in coolness, and the cottagers are unwilling to go indoors and shut themselves in their small bedrooms, where the windows, though unusually wide open, admit little air and even the bedside candle has wilted with the heat. Only the children, reprieved from the sentence of bedtime, find enough energy to shout and play: their parents lean over gates and hedges, talking to neighbours across the way, or occupy the favourite cottage view-point of a chair just inside the open door. Habit rather than desire sends all indoors at last, with low "good-nights" and a clicking of gate latches and a turning of enormous keys in the doors. Bats flicker and stars shine, but it is not silence yet: voices in the low bedrooms can still be heard as last words are exchanged before turning to an uneasy sleep. . . . And just one more such instance, this time from that second country harvest when the corn is all ingathered and the labourer turns to the garnering of his own crops, the roots and fruits of garden and allotment. In one garden there is the pungent smell of feathery carrot-tops, as these are chopped off and the roots themselves thrown on the ground to dry. In another the last touches are being put to a clamp down at the far end—a neat affair like an igloo with a small straw chimney. Much simple pride went to the making of this clamp. First a round basin was dug in the ground and lined with straw. This was then filled with the carrots, each laid with its tapering rootlet towards the centre. When the whole crop had been built into a domed heap, more straw was laid on, and earth shovelled over all, leaving only a straw vent at the top. Finally, the clamp was wetted and patted down with a spade, trim and ship-shape, and a narrow trench, complete with run-away, opened all round. So the valuable crop is safeguarded against weather and vermin, to be opened as need be in the difficult months ahead.

But perhaps, after all, the best way in which I can hope to convey something of this cottage economy will be to tell of a particular cottage I knew fairly intimately as a boy—that time of life when, though we are unaware of it, we are receptive to detail as we never shall be again. Once every year I was taken to stay for a while with my paternal grandparents. Their diminutive cottage was already well on the way to being swallowed in the suburbs of the nearby town, and now it has disappeared altogether. But when I pass that way to-day in the train, as I sometimes do, it is not so much the sprawling town that I see from the carriage windows, with its congestion of houses and hardly a tree between, as my grandparents' tiny cottage, with its country smells and country ways—as if this would endure, in memory, when all these boxes of brick and mortar shall have fallen apart.

From the outside the cottage was nothing to look at: brick walls abutting on to the busy road, small windows out of which to peer at the passing traffic, and a slate roof. But even from the outside some hint was given of the neatness within by the flowered lace curtains and clean glass and whitened doorstep. All the garden was at the back of the cottage. It consisted of a long strip of ground, down the whole length of which, close against the dividing hedge of trim quick, ran a cobbled path. Never a weed was allowed to grow between those smooth, shiny cobbles that glistened in the rain and composed as good a garden path as any I have known.

COTTAGE AT BURGHCLERE, HAMPSHIRE
Detail from an oil painting by Stanley Spencer

When he was over seventy, my grandfather would still get down on his knees (protected with a folded sack which he dragged with him inch by inch up the path) and dig out each tiny blade of grass with an old horn-handled dinner knife. Bordering the cobbled path there was a long row of clove carnations, my grandfather's pride and joy; and even to-day nothing will bring back the memory of that little garden, with its simple husbandry, like the fragrance of these favourite flowers.

Inside, everything was speckless—which is not at all to say that my grandmother was house-proud at the expense of full living: she was, indeed, within her necessarily narrow circumstances, as avid for experience as a bee for honey: it was simply that untidiness and its accompanying dirt would have meant confusion, and my grandparents could not afford confusion. I used to sleep in a little bedroom at the back of the cottage, and if I hung my head over the side of the bed I could just manage to see out of the window that was set almost at floor level. I would be wakened in the morning by the sounds of activity below—the pumping and splashing of water, the clatter of pans, the sizzling of bacon, the chatter of morning voices. Nothing was said or done in that cottage which could not be heard everywhere: one could also hear most of what went on next door. Intimacy, in fact, is the very characteristic of such cottages; and whilst, in some instances, it may lead to coarseness and sluttery, in others it leads to orderliness and a general simplicity of behaviour: it all depends upon the essential nature of the cottagers concerned. Everything in its place and a place for everything: this is a sheer necessity in cottage life. Thus, through the generations, these limitations of space, coupled with small earnings, have induced in the best kind of cottager a ritual of conduct based on neatness and simplicity: a discipline having its foundation in compulsion but none the less admirable in effect for that. To the cottager of the good old school, waste was a major sin.

But the room I remember best in my grandparents' cottage was the little front room. It was work-room, living-room, dining-room, parlour, and everything else. I marvel now when I think of the multitude of activities it adapted itself to in the course of the week without once losing that modest dignity and comfort which were the unspoken pleasure of all who entered it. These might range from squire to roadman, parson to grocer's boy: whoever they were, they could not help but feel at home the moment they entered. It seems to me as if, whenever I was there, a continual flow of visitors of one sort or another came into that little room. Perhaps my grandmother, seated in her wheelback armchair in the chimney corner, would be shelling a bowl of peas in her lap. Whatever she was doing, she never laid aside her task for long out of deference to a caller. The routine of the morning must go its accustomed way, or she would never get through all the things that had to be done before the day was out. Nor did she ever apologise: indeed, there was no need. Peeling potatoes or polishing the grate, ironing shirts or pouring out tea, she ever maintained that natural dignity which is beyond the prerogative of class. Quality, I realise to-day, was the hall-mark of the tiny cottage and all that went on there. It proclaimed itself even in the cottage furniture—the polished tripod table, smooth as glass, the corner cupboard, with its lustre jug and Lowestoft china, the old carved chest, smelling of lavender bags when it was opened, the severe wooden chairs, well-turned and comely, and the grandfather clock wheezing in the corner. But most it proclaimed itself in the owners and users of these things.

Somehow it was my grandmother who, all day, dominated the scene. Perhaps the reason for this was simply that, in the daytime, my grandfather would be out and about a great deal. But when evening came he took the centre of the simple stage. With her hands folded quiet at last on her black silk apron and her evening lace cap on her head, my grandmother would sit attentively listening while he read aloud to her. Invariably those readings followed the same course: a bit or two out of the newspaper, a letter that must be read over again and discussed, and then, to finish up with, a few pages from a favourite book. I do not suppose there were more than half a dozen books all told in that cottage, for the only schooling the old couple had ever known was a dame school for which their parents paid a penny or two a week. And of that half-dozen I am only certain now of one.

'WILL IT RAIN?'
Oil painting by J. Charles, 1887

It always seems to have been the same book from which my grandfather read, at least when I was there. I did not know much about the meaning of faith in those days, but now I should not hesitate to say that my grandparents were its humble and whole-hearted exponents. And I think it must have been the fervour and actuality which my grandfather managed to put into his reading of the trials and endurances of Christian that has identified Bunyan's immortal book with him in my mind, so that all the well-known passages seem to say themselves to me in his voice, the while

I see my grandmother sitting by, listening, her eyes curtained behind their delicately veined lids. "Then I saw in my dream, that on the morrow he got up to go forwards, but they desired him to stay till the next day also; and then, said they, we will (if the day be clear) show you the Delectable Mountains; which, they said, would yet farther add to his comfort, because they were nearer the desired haven, than the place where at present he was: so he consented and staid. When the morning was up, they had him to the top of the house, and bid him look south: so he did; and behold, at a great distance, he saw a most pleasant mountainous country, beautified with woods, vine-yards, fruits of all sorts, flowers also, with springs and fountains, very delectable to behold. Then he asked the name of the country: they said, it was Emanuel's Land!"

SIXTEENTH-CENTURY THATCHED COTTAGE
Drawing by John Crome, 1768-1821

SHORT BIBLIOGRAPHY

The Development of English Building Construction by C. F. Innocent. 1916, Cambridge University Press.—*The English Cottage* by Harry Batsford and Charles Fry. 1938, Batsford.—*The Story of the English House* by Hugh Brown. 1940, Batsford.—*The Roof Tree* by James Kenward. 1938, Oxford University Press.—*In Bucks* by G. Eland. 1923, G. T. de Fraine & Co., Aylesbury.—*Change in the Farm* by Thomas Hennell. 1934, Cambridge University Press.—*The Village Carpenter* by Walter Rose. 1937, Cambridge University Press.—*The Bettesworth Book* by George Bourne. 1901, London.—*Lucy Bettesworth* by George Bourne. 1913, Duckworth.—Books by Richard Jefferies, especially *The Toilers of the Field* (1892), *Field and Hedgerow* (1889), and *Hodge and his Masters* (1880).—*The Wayfarer's Companion* by Arnold Fellows. 1937, Oxford University Press